For Julianna, with thanks
—M.L.

Spots, by Marcia Leonard, photographs by Dorothy Handelman.
Copyright © 1998 by The Millbrook Press Inc.
Reprinted by arrangement with The Millbrook Press, Inc.

Houghton Mifflin Edition, 2005

Printed in the U.S.A.

ISBN: 0-618-06184-3

56789-B-06 05 04 03

Spots

By **Marcia Leonard**
Photographs by **Dorothy Handelman**

HOUGHTON MIFFLIN   BOSTON · MORRIS PLAINS, NJ

California · Colorado · Georgia · Illinois · New Jersey · Texas

I like spots.
I like them lots.

5

I like spots that are big.
I like spots that are small.

7

I like spots that are blots.
But that is not all.

I have a lamp with spots.

I have a rug with spots.

I sip my milk
from a mug with spots.

15

I like spots on a dog.
I like spots on a ball.

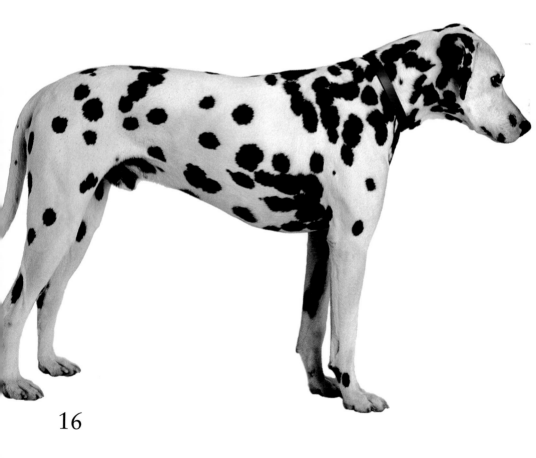

17

I like spots on a bug.
But that is not all.

I have a hat with spots.

21

I have a dress with spots.

23

And just for fun,
I make a mess with spots.

I like to put
all my spots in one spot.

Oh, yes! I like spots.

My twin sister does not!